Fantastic Creations

Edited By Holly Sheppard

First published in Great Britain in 2020 by:

Young Writers
Remus House
Coltsfoot Drive
Peterborough
PE2 9BF
Telephone: 01733 890066
Website: www.youngwriters.co.uk

Printed and bound in the UK by BookPrintingUK
Website: www.bookprintinguk.com
YB0432U

FOREWORD

Hello Reader!

For our latest poetry competition we sent out funky and vibrant worksheets for primary school pupils to fill in and create their very own poem about fiendish fiends and crazy creatures. I got to read them and guess what? They were **roarsome**!

The pupils were able to read our example poems and use the fun-filled free resources to help bring their imaginations to life, and the result is pages **oozing** with exciting poetic tales. From friendly monsters to mean monsters, from bumps in the night to **rip-roaring** adventures, these pupils have excelled themselves, and now have the joy of seeing their work in print!

Here at Young Writers we love nothing more than poetry and creativity. We aim to encourage children to put pen to paper to inspire a love of the written word and explore their own unique worlds of creativity. We'd like to congratulate all of the aspiring authors that have created this book of **monstrous mayhem** and we know that these poems will be enjoyed for years to come. So, dive on in and submerge yourself in all things furry and fearsome (and perhaps check under the bed!).

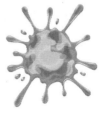

CONTENTS

Connie-Leigh Stant (10)	60
Kayleigh McGinty (10)	61
Finley Baker (10)	62
Keelee Natasha Zupan-Turner (10)	63
Kellan Smith (9)	64
Alecia Bethany Martina Sitton (9)	65
Gracie Kadar (10)	66
Charlotte Kelly (9)	67
Natasha Eva Ford (10)	68
Isobelle Clay (11)	69
Maisy Murray (10)	70
Dylan Ashton Desmond (10)	71
Lilly Amanda (10)	72
Charlie Pearce (10)	73
Bryoni Maria Homatopoulos (9)	74
Lydia Mcdonough (10)	75
Olivia Tunnicliffe (10)	76
Daniel Kirk (9)	77
Evee Harding-Double (9)	78
Miles Martin (9)	79
Billy Henry Sharpe (9)	80
Lily Sandra Grave Andrews (9)	81
Cara-Leigh Tyler (10)	82

Langlands Primary School, Forfar

Lexi Smith (9)	83
Zoë McGregor (10)	84
Louie Gowans (10)	86
Jordan Walker (10)	88
Jasmine Bell (10)	90
Jay Elder (10)	92
Erin Anderson (10)	94
Holli Smith (10)	95
Ashlyn Smith (10)	96
Maya McInnes (10)	97
Ellie Jane Thomson (10)	98
Craig Murray (10)	99
Kathryn Gould (9)	100
Thea Forbes (10)	101
Caitlyn Brogan (10)	102
Logan Byrne (10)	103

Wiktoria Tomaczowska (9)	104

Madni Academy, Savile Town

Mariam Enany (11)	105
Aima Malik (9)	106
Fatima Malik (11)	108
Hibba Anis (10)	110
Amaara Bukhari (9)	111
Aaminah Ejaz (11)	112
Khadeejah Salaam (9)	113
Wissal Graiaouni (10)	114
Habiba Shah (10)	115
Zonaira Dar (10)	116
Roqayyah Bint Ziaullah (10)	117
Maryam Amankwah (10)	118

Parent Concern, Cheadle

Kyle Barnett (9)	119
George Harrison (8)	120
Alfie Moore (10)	121
Luke Seed (10)	122

St Edward's CE Primary School, Castleton

Finlay Rowan (8)	123
David Rami Erdogan (8)	124
Cole Brooks (9)	125
Keona Chiwanda (8)	126
Lexie Rae Kathleen Mcgarry (8)	127
Lewis Pattinson (8)	128
Kelis Idaewor-Knox (8)	129

St. Peter's Primary School, South Croydon

Libby Wade (9)	130

Ummul Mumineen Academy, Grangetown

Hannah Ebrahim (11)	131
Zaynah Miznah Hussein (8)	132

Yarm School, Yarm

Katie Cheesman (8)	133
Edie Redhead Sweeney (8)	134

Ysgol Gymraeg Bro Allta, Ystrad Mynach

Grace Broe (8)	135
Elena Bilenki (8)	136
Abigail Roberts (8)	138
Jac Davies (8)	140
Heulyn Philip Webb Price (8)	142
Elektra Clarke (7)	144
Dylan Rourke (9)	145
Dylan Teconi (8)	146
Harrison Gray Martin (8)	148
Cariad Morgan (7)	149
Llewelyn Cribb (8)	150
Elan Davies (9)	151
Kyle Gittings (7)	152
Caitlin Elizabeth Bosher-Lewis (9)	153
Osian Evans (8)	154
Seren Croll (8)	155
Aidan Lloyd Williams (8)	156
Gethin Marsh (9)	157
Imogen Wivell (8)	158
Logan Barwood (9)	159
Kian John Kevan Inseal (8)	160
Lilly-May Sullivan (8)	161
Elisa Ruth Poole (8)	162
Evie-Louise Corns (8)	163
Morgan Daniel (9)	164
Phoebe Holland (8)	165
Isabelle Louise McBride (9)	166
Ioan Roberts (8)	167
Carys Rhianwen Mair Davies (8)	168

Harri Ap Llwyd Dafydd (7)	169
Lexie Cox (7)	170
Dylan D'Cruz (7)	171
Abi-Mai Yendle (8)	172
Lucas Owen Yeo (8)	173
Joseph Anthony Gill (8)	174
Ben Tomas Watkins (8)	175
Mali Dummett (8)	176
Harlow Amelia Nicholas (7)	177
Ffion Francis (8)	178
Leila-Jo Powell (9)	179
Blaidd Carwyn Clifford (8)	180
Abigail Lucy Brown (9)	181
Aimee Harris (9)	182
Olivia Morris-Brown (8)	183
Amelia Angel (7)	184
Thomas Clutton (8)	185
Iolo Anthony (8)	186
Lois Poole (8)	187
Dylan Jones (8)	188
Tieghan White (9)	189
Niamh Protheroe	190
William Chant (7)	191
Lennon Hughes (8)	192
Taylor Jay Jones (8)	193
Mia Saunders (8)	194
Nathaniel Sears (8)	195
Summer Cushing (8)	196

THE POEMS

Ghost-Blob

My monster's name is Ghost-Blob
When I think of him I quietly sob
He is as fast as speedy Flash
If you want to hurt him, give him a bash!
He is very slimy with lots of slime
He takes things and he says, "That's mine!"
He is really angry and crushes things
He hates people who sing
He will destroy a city
But he gets confused when he sees a kitty
He is evil in his evil lair
His favourite fruit has always been pear
One day he came to me
I tried to run free
He wanted to do me harm
I saw him, he just crushed a farm
I hope he doesn't come again
I barely made it out alive
All the bees were attacking him
They want to protect their hive.

Jenson Pilbrow (7)
Ashford Park Primary School, Ashford

The Nightmare Cyclops Devil

The Nightmare Cyclops Devil sucks good dreams
And replaces them with bad dreams
The Nightmare Cyclops Devil is friends with
Ice Spike, The Stitch, Ghost Blob and Mr Loury.

His enemies are Love Hug and Bubble Hug
Bubble Hug replaces bad dreams with good
dreams
He is as furious as a bull
He has a hundred legs as thin as pencils
He has six arms like tentacles
When he eats the dreams
He makes a Gobolob sound
Everyone is scared of his huge fangs
His burning hot horns shine like rubies
His body red like a poppy
He is misunderstood
Because the dreams are about climate change.

Sophia Poppy Sanderson (8)
Ashford Park Primary School, Ashford

Happy Scarlet

My monster is Scarlet
She is a nice monster and so kind
Scarlet is tall as a mansion
She tries to not break anything
When she walks, it makes a *boom, boom,* sound
She has three hands and three heads
And six eyes
My monster has hair like a person
My monster is like a spotty monster
She has so much fluff so much fluff so people can
hug her
And be warm
When it is night-time
She makes so much noise
She sleeps under the bed
And sometimes she snores
She has black eyes
That are as shiny as diamonds.

Husna Behsudi (7)
Ashford Park Primary School, Ashford

The Stitch

Stitch is a monster that listens to dreams
She is as tiny as a toe
She is as small as an ant
She likes to eat dreams and pizza
She helps people's dreams, good or bad
She is as high as a cloud
She lives in the town of Simber
She has two friends
Number one is called Nightmare Cyclops Devil
She is spiky and makes nightmares
Her second friend is called Bubble Hug
Beware, beware of these monsters
Together they all fight
Stitch is noble and independent
She is as smart as a dolphin.

Jessica Howe (8)
Ashford Park Primary School, Ashford

Bubble Hug, The Two-Headed Monster

Bubble Hug is as soft as a bear
She's kind
She loves bubbles.

She likes to eat McDonald's
She likes chocolate
She likes vegetables.

She takes away bad dreams
But replaces them with good dreams
Bubbling with craziness like a bubble machine
When she's jumping about, the Earth goes boom.

She has a spotty couch
She likes tidying her room
She likes wearing long skirts
She's got short, sticky tentacles
Razor-sharp horns.

Evie Killick (8)
Ashford Park Primary School, Ashford

The Three-Headed Monster

The Three-Headed Monster is funny
He is kind
He does not pick up his toys
He does not make his bed
He is mighty and dangerous
He has lots of eyes
His favourite colour is gold
His favourite sports are cricket and football
He is thirteen years old
He is as slippery as a snake
He has a coach for cricket
He is scary
He is terrifying
He is creepy
He has three heads
He is green
He has green eyes
He has green fur

He can flip
He can do gymnastics.

Charles William Ledger (8)

Ashford Park Primary School, Ashford

Playful Bob

If you are nice a little monster might come
If you are sad, Bob will cheer you up
I will play anything
If you are bad he will gobble you up whole
He might let you come to his house only if he is
feeling good
He can see 100 miles if you need help
He can fight a giant if he hurts you
Bob can let bees free if they are hurting you
He will get you a pet and take it to the vet
When he needs help
He goes boom and shoots out goo.

Henry Slater (7)
Ashford Park Primary School, Ashford

Dobby The Monster

My name is Dobby
I like to do my hobby
I love to play basketball
I love to play football
I have a big hairy beard
And I wish to be weird
I have a tiny red eye
That likes to eat pie
I have ears as big as pizza slices
I like to eat woodlice
Lob is my friend
I like to lend
When I draw it hurts my paw
I like to saw
When I whoosh
I tell my partner to shhh
When my zip is stuck
I get bad luck!

Annie Bell (8)
Ashford Park Primary School, Ashford

Dugly Who Lives In Your School

This is Dugly
He is really nosey
And he sneaks into your bedroom
His favourite thing is scaring people
He is as hungry as a lion
And is as deadly as a tiger
He creeps into the cupboard until night
He is a nosey, messy monster
So beware and hide under your covers
Make sure he doesn't come into your bedroom
He is as big as an elephant
And as quick as a bee
He has six big tentacles
And jumps like a flea.

Joshua Charlie Lawrence (8)
Ashford Park Primary School, Ashford

Deadly Poem!

This is Blue Dead
When he's under the children's beds
His deadly eyes turn blood-red
He lives in a volcano
He doesn't like tornadoes
He has blue, shiny, crystal-clear skin
He likes to have treats
He doesn't like sweets
He might look deadly but he's harmless
He's not too big or too small
He's the size of a human
He likes to eat prawns
He doesn't have claws
Beware! Beware!

Maya Rapa (8)
Ashford Park Primary School, Ashford

Scary Monster

This is Scary Simon
Simon is as fierce as a shark
Simon is as scary as a lion
His nose can *snap!*
He can spell spellings easily
He is the smartest in the world
He might even take his eyeballs out
He can widen his eyes
He might even be a spelling king
He might even be a times table hero
He can turn invisible
He can turn enormous
He is cuter than a unicorn
He is so enormous.

Ashwin Sarvananthan (7)
Ashford Park Primary School, Ashford

Scary Monster

This is Scary Simon
Simon is as fierce as a shark
Simon is as scary as a lion
He can snap his nose
He can widen his eyes
He can spell spellings so crazy
He is the smartest in the world
He might even take his eyeballs out
He might even be a spelling king
He might even be a times table hero
He can turn invisible
He is cuter than a unicorn
He is smelly
He is enormous.

Jayden Dunham (7)
Ashford Park Primary School, Ashford

Craft Craw

His dad is called Ark
He raps but not in the dark
So he never gets caught
People think he's rude
But he's actually kind
He's very smart
He's very very fluffy
He's fluffier than a teddy.

He's creative too
He makes costumes to disguise himself in
He is as slow as a snail
He's as smart as Einstein
He's as scary as a ghost.

Jayden Turner (8)
Ashford Park Primary School, Ashford

Big Black Spider

This is Weird Spider
His big black body jumps
He has seventeen eyes
He is as hungry as a million giant squids
He is as dark as night
Spiders wings whoosh in the air
He can go a hundred miles per hour
He is hairy and scary
But he is kind
His belly is a bottomless pit
The eyes on his face can see through anything
He is big and fluffy
Will you be his friend?

Aladin Abaraou (7)
Ashford Park Primary School, Ashford

Spike Slime

Hi, my name is Spike
My eyes pop out when I am happy
I am as big as a whale
I am as green as grass
I am as strong as an elephant
I am as soft as a pillow
At night I am out crossing streets
Leaving slime tracks over the place
I am creepy so watch out
I might see you
I am quiet and scary
I wonder if I'll visit you
I am very scary, boo!

Adam Ferreira-Kallat (7)
Ashford Park Primary School, Ashford

Spiky The Evil Werewolf

This is Spiky
His ears are as pointy as a werewolf's
You might want to hide
Or you might die
He has red spiky hair
He has red eyes like blood
And he has sharp pointy nails
So be careful!
He is very dangerous
If you see him you will scream
He can hear from a mile away
So don't talk at night
Or he will give you a fright!

Heidi Francis (7)
Ashford Park Primary School, Ashford

Greedy Ollie

Greedy Ollie is a smelly monster
He likes jumping slowly everywhere
He's as big as an elephant
And he can breathe fire out of his nose.

He bangs and crashes
He pounds the hard ground
He never takes a bath
He doesn't want to sleep.

He stays up all night
Greedy Ollie wears a black dress
With a stripe.

Agamveer Chandhok (7)

Ashford Park Primary School, Ashford

This Is Olive

This is Olive
His nose is as big as his head
He calls everything 'bog roll' and 'peanut'
Bogies come out of his nose every second
He smells like a twit
His hair is like a blue triangle
He only has two fingers
He hated the others so he cut them off
Most importantly, he's always naked.

Harvey Jackson (7)
Ashford Park Primary School, Ashford

This Is Doggy

This is Doggy!
He's as tough as iron.

He has sharp pointy nails;
That could rip you into half.

He is extremely scary;
So no one goes near him.

He is as smelly as a rotten fish;
So it may often need a bath.

If someone tries to sneaks up on him;
He will eat them up!

Hafid Mohamed (7)
Ashford Park Primary School, Ashford

Hungry Clumsy

I am pretty clumsy
I am sad because I am hungry
I have three eyes that are clumsy
My tummy rumbles every second
I have smelly eyes that eat food
I see yummy foods that are yummy
I taste my delicious lasagne
I drink lovely lemonade
My favourite drink is lemonade
You should try it.

Aila Choudry (7)
Ashford Park Primary School, Ashford

Crit Creet

This is Crit Creet
He can't eat
He has big, rough spiky legs
That are as white as eggs
He's as evil as a shark
That can bark
Crit Creet sings as loud as a balloon pop
He's always moaning
But not frowning
He writes neat
And is always dancing to the beat.

Samuel Torres (7)
Ashford Park Primary School, Ashford

Bogey

This is Bogey
He is as slimy as a bogey
He is as smelly as a rotten banana skin
He has pointy green hair like green snot
Sometimes he wrecks stuff like bins
It makes a *bang* noise
He is extremely stinky
Everybody has to hold their nose
His behaviour is not good.

Rhys Pankhania (7)

Ashford Park Primary School, Ashford

Tiny Tim

This is Tiny Tim
He's as small as a toddler
His snot always drips down
He has spikes on his head
That he will spike you with
He is extremely lonely
Will you play with him?
He has spiky teeth
Teeth that have blood on them
He lives in the toilet.

Ella Fitzpatrick (7)
Ashford Park Primary School, Ashford

Gowe

He has eyes as green as leaves
He is dangerously cute
He has soft fur
He loves girl monsters
He does flips to impress the girls
He is as handsome as a prince
He's got sharp teeth as white as a sheep
He's got red eyes
As bright as a burning fire.

Henry Heath (7)
Ashford Park Primary School, Ashford

Mr Lowy, Miss Snowy And Bowy

Mr Lowy, Miss Snowy and Bowy
Are the biggest monsters in monster town
They are really helpful
They love to eat snow as cold as ice
They have thirty-eight eyes
They bring beautiful dreams
Mr Lowy is blue
Miss Snowy is pink
Bowy is as purple as violets.

Amelia Jedreasz (7)
Ashford Park Primary School, Ashford

Infinity Monster

He is as old as thirty-one years old
But he wants to be older
He gets stuck in bed
When he starts to tread
He jumps as high as a trampoline
He is as small as a mouse
He has twenty-two terrific spikes
He has little legs like a centipede.

Alfie Thomas (7)
Ashford Park Primary School, Ashford

Booppy Poppy

Poppy is mean to other monsters
She is really cold like an ice cube
Poppy has really spiky hair
She has really small poky arms
Poppy is really fierce like a tiger
She has little sharp teeth
Poppy is terrifying like a lion.

Savannah Ovenell (7)

Ashford Park Primary School, Ashford

Suty

This is Suty
He's furry like a pillow
He's got a friend called Willow
He's got shiny eyes to see in the dark
Do you want to be his friend?
I will because he's furry like a teddy
And he is friendly.

Lucja Bochynska (8)

Ashford Park Primary School, Ashford

Happy

This is Happy
Happy is a very friendly monster
He is as blue as the sky
He is as soft as a pillow
Do you want a monster like Happy?
If you want a monster like Happy
Then you need to be happy.

Irina Bushan (7)
Ashford Park Primary School, Ashford

Dog Zombies Rule

I'm smelly
I'm hairy
My ears are floppy
I am disgusting and slimy
I sound like a pig snoring
I thump and bump
I jump like a frog
I roar like thunder
I stomp up the street.

Michael Darby
Ashford Park Primary School, Ashford

Bob The Creature

This is Bob
Bob isn't very friendly at all
If you touch him
He will bite your fingers off
His nose is very pointy
He is as sneaky as a ninja
But he still isn't very friendly at all.

Alexandra Maria Tomulescu (8)
Ashford Park Primary School, Ashford

Boby

Boby loves bobbing in the sea
Boby loves eating fish
He likes to find crazy fish
He looks like a monster
He has not got a lot of friends in the sea
He is a crazy man
He is violent.

Callum Smith (7)

Ashford Park Primary School, Ashford

Spiky

He has spikes as sharp as a knife
He has legs as red as fire
When he walks
He is as silent as a mouse
If you see him
He is friendly
Spiky has the sense of smell of a lion.

Jack Collins (7)
Ashford Park Primary School, Ashford

Snotter

This is Snotter
He is as dirty as a bin
He is as smelly as rotten eggs
He is as fast as a cheetah
He eats as much as elephants
He has a green nose.

Lillie Beecher
Ashford Park Primary School, Ashford

Spiky Snot

Spiky Snot is very spiky
He even has spikes under his nose
He has entrancing flames on his head
If you go under your bed
He will spike you every day!

Sophie James (8)
Ashford Park Primary School, Ashford

My Monster

My monster is big and scary
And he is very hairy
One of his heads will eat you up
The head on his neck will throw out some
creatures
And eat all of you up
He breaks your jaw
And strangles you.

Trystan Wyse (8)
Bargeddie Primary School, Bargeddie

Spooky Den

Spooky Den lives in a cave
He likes laughing a lot
My monster has fluff all around him
He is the colour of a rainbow.

Skye Leigh Dunsmore (7)
Bargeddie Primary School, Bargeddie

Doughnut The Beast

D arius walked down the stairs with a feeling of dread

O n his shoulders was a head... that he should have used

U sually Darius would have checked with his parents before he went downstairs after hearing footsteps

G *o into the kitchen,* he thought, but his logic told him otherwise

H e stepped cautiously into the kitchen and saw

N othing

U ntil

T he great fat beast was stood in front of him! Clobbering feet and sharp claws, a big belly and massive eyes. Her drool made Darius retch. In her hand was a doughnut. Just a doughnut. Nothing else.

Louis Insull (10)
Birkdale Preparatory School, Sheffield

The Eloniese

My monster can fly higher than the universe
He has a big tail and at the end of it
Is a huge poisonous stinger
It has a big mane all made of ice
His weakness is lots of light
When he has waited for the dead of night
He eats all of the children who had nice dreams
As he opens his mouth
He reveals a huge circular tongue
He lives in the centre of the Earth's core
His tail can change from a poisonous stinger
To a deadly drill or a huge sword
But there is a huge blaster that he can use
His name is Eloniese.

Lenny Patel (7)
Birkdale Preparatory School, Sheffield

Nation Monster (Cricket)

A monster who will support any nation from far
and wide
Sneaky as a sly fox
You might want to know where he is
He might already be right next to you
Gigantic, fat, disgusting mouth
His tongue is as white as a cloud
Jammie Dodgers are his favourite snack
He eats them every day
Monstrous, humungous monster
With a huge heart
Super at hide-and-seek
That's his favourite game
Tremendously cute and small for a monster
Tremendous shot for a cricket player.

Aadam Akram (10)
Birkdale Preparatory School, Sheffield

The Zombie King

My monster's wings flap about helpless
He sometimes flies
But his old age gets the best of him
His toenails are so long
He has to laser them every two years
His crown is as rusty as a piece of old battered
metal mesh
His jet boosters boost him high and far
His tongue is made from pure dried poison
He has scars all over his body
From the battles he has won
He is pure god though (don't tell anyone).

Austin Campbell-Pilling (9)
Birkdale Preparatory School, Sheffield

Herrmitom The Great

H ealthy, evil and anxious, crawling in the dark

E nvious of absolute angels

R eeks of evil but innocence

R uns away from dragons in disguise

M ean, mad, malicious and malevolent

I nside madness rages

T urning into a mad professor

O n his back are the wings of a goddess

M oving in the midnight sky, his infrared vision will catch you off guard.

Reuben Heath Barnett (11)

Birkdale Preparatory School, Sheffield

Shemlond

S caly as a komodo dragon
H ealthy as a doctor's oldest patient
E xotic as a poison dart frog
M agical as a wizard
L ong as a hundred worms
O bnoxious as a fox
N ever been treated well
D eadly as a spinosaurus.

Noah Carr (8)
Birkdale Preparatory School, Sheffield

Gaffer Whiskers

An eyeball like a minion's eye
Scraped knees like football shinpads
He is hairy as a lion's mane
His fingertips are as sharp as needles
He's bigger than a giant's tummy
He's as loud as Mr Noisy
He is stronger than the Incredible Hulk!

Zoubin Jackson (7)
Birkdale Preparatory School, Sheffield

The Gruzzle

Maintenance man Mike dragged his feet along the
corridor
Abruptly stopping at the door
Noisily, he thumped the blockade
Faces glared at him from inside
And the half-destroyed package that he carried
Students pondered what was hidden inside the
bruised box.

Ding-a-ling! A ling! Breaktime!
The harsh sound ripped through the air
Boys flooded out the door
With a sly smile and licking his lips
Adrian levitated the straps and sellotape
Off the brown box.

Eyes like stars
Soft as a well-loved bear
Colour demon
Small boy-like cheeky smile
The Gruzzle glared.

It bounded up
Yanked the boy's bright blue blazer
With globe-like eyes, The Gruzzle scanned the room
The monster was hungry for colour
He craved the rainbow wonders around him
Contrasting the bleak, grey world he came from.

He spotted the bright pencil gems
Sleeping soundly in a boy's pocket
Like a spirit possessed
The Gruzzle grabbed the loot
That spewed out like lava
And stuffed it into his skin sack.

Stunned, shocked, surprised
Adrian assumed karate left guard
He wasn't giving up his pencils without a fight
Like cowboys, the two mammals' eyes met
Ears filled with fighting theme tunes
The Gruzzle made its move, going for the flame-like curls
But The Ginger Ninja was on his toes

Dodged the flying fury
Letting it sail safely into the battered box.

Slam, slap, stick
The Gruzzle was safely sealed
Booming footsteps
Echoed down the hallway
Mrs Parker paused, sidled over to Adrian
Slyly winked, "Ah, I see you've found our new class pet!"

Freddie Snowball (9)
Eaton House The Manor School, Clapham

The Sneakeater

Beware of The Sneakeater
Softly he creeps
Sneakily he moves
Through your bedroom door
His clawed feet scrape across the floor
The spikes on his tail are sticky with blood
He is not discriminating
He steals all human prey.

Beware of The Sneakeater
He'll eat you alive
With horns as sharp as knives
And eyes gleaming like lava
Wait! Do you hear the scratching?
Crash!
He is here...

Freddy Tinworth (9)
Eaton House The Manor School, Clapham

Pinkaboo

As this beast came out of my cupboard
Pink was everywhere around me
With ginormous spots
His horn was as sharp as a knife
His eyes were as black as the night
The monster came closer and closer
As I hid under my cover, I felt his hands.

Then I heard him jump onto my bed
With his hands still on me
He was as smelly as someone
Who hadn't showered for a week
He opened his big mouth
And did a humungous slurp
His fangs didn't even fit in his mouth
He grabbed hold of my cover and pulled it
Then I saw him eye to eye.

I started shouting for my mum
But it was no use
I started to wish for the bed
To swallow me up.

He got closer and closer
I kept on going backwards when I couldn't any
more
I banged my head on the wall
But there was more to think about
Then my mum opened the door
And the monster disappeared!

Jack Catterall (10)
Eaton House The Manor School, Clapham

Buggy

Just a few years ago
There was a monster as fat as a hippo
He went by the name Buggy
Buggy always goes around scaring people
He normally had at least ten gallons of blood
On his teeth
Buggy had fangs as sharp as the tip of a star
And he ran like a Ferarri.

One huge eye as gigantic as the sun
The voices of people would be heard by Buggy
From ten miles away
He was aggressive and deadly
Even the white shark isn't as dangerous as Buggy
He was 100% rubber
He never got a scratch.

He was lonely and sensitive
He would get you
Especially if you said no to his friend requests
Or if you said something about his face
Buggy was bullied so much.

His frightening head was worth a fortune
He got called mean names
Anywhere
Everywhere
But all he really wanted was a friend.

Mark Flavin (9)

Eaton House The Manor School, Clapham

The Doppelgänger

"There he is
The Doppelgänger
Everywhere yet nowhere
The cruellest beast
With no room for a heart,"
They all say.

Horns like knives
And claws like razors
They don't know the real me
The considerate me
The fun me
Me.

Angus Ludgate (9)
Eaton House The Manor School, Clapham

Ted From In The Hedge

I can see something from in the hedge
I can see his horns and head
And the CWC merch he has on
I can see his big brown head
I can smell the grass in the garden
At night, I sneak out of my room
He's not in the hedge
But stood before me
And he's called Ted.

I can see the food Ted has eaten
From Dad's secret sweet tin
Too many E numbers, he's wriggling
I can see his eyes, all two of them
I can feel his fur
I can see his shoes, Nikes
Ted is my friend
I wake up in the morning and see him in daylight
He scares me sometimes
He looks scared
His fur is caught on the thorn bush
Sometimes he eats the fruit from the bushes.

Ryan James Weller (9)
Harwich Community Primary School & Nursery, Harwich

Lurking Under Your Bed!

She's waiting for you
To come to bed
You'll get stuck between her jaws
You'll get hurt when she sees you.

She loves having children for dinner
They're her favourite treat
She's waiting for you
You'll get trapped between her fangs
She creeps under your bed when you're asleep.

She's waiting for you to come home from school
To trap you in her cave
She's waiting to eat you up whole
She eats all of your clothes
She's as scary as a snake!

She's eaten you up whole
You were very crunchy
Snap! Snap! Snap!
She moves to another bed
To eat another child

Kodie Sharpe (10)
Harwich Community Primary School & Nursery, Harwich

Scaly

The slithering scaly monster
Lives within the muddy lake
Hunting down its prey
Flying over trees, burning them to ash
Like a fire bird.

When you see this monster
Make sure you don't make a peep
Or you will be trapped between its jaws.

It sits there waiting, waiting, waiting
Waiting for the right time
Beware of this creature
Its crystal-clear eyes can look
Right through your soul.

If it catches you
There is no escape
It will haunt you
Till the monster
Has a taste of your blood.

Teale Rose Jones (10)
Harwich Community Primary School & Nursery, Harwich

My Monster, Dave

My monster is a smelly chap
He smells like mouldy cheese
He has big long hairy toes
And bunions on his knees
He lives in a cave full of mould
And his favourite drink is boiled bogey tea
That he drinks cold.

He loves to bathe in a muddy swamp
And when he walks he makes a stomp
He likes to dine on beetles and ants
Which sometimes escape and he finds them in his
pants.

Despite all these peculiar habits
He has a heart full of gold
He is a very helpful friend to have
And he is also very bold.

Chloe Polaine (10)
Harwich Community Primary School & Nursery, Harwich

Mr Horny

The scary monster can hear you wherever you are
He lives in a trench
And he likes to kill rats
His arms are like bats
He sees the flamethrower
He will say to the soldiers to get lower.

Mustard gas he has, ready to kill
You can see it about to get thrown over the hill
Better run before you get killed
One soldier drowned in the mustard gas
It was a terrible sight.

The monster got scared
When he got told to be aware
He had to keep watch
In the trench
Luckily, no one came by.

Alfie Heath (10)
Harwich Community Primary School & Nursery, Harwich

Cute But Vicious!

You will be tricked with her cuteness
But inside she is vicious
She hates children
When they play with her
She takes them and kills them
She says that they ran off to their parents
You are probably wondering what her name is
It's Mia
So parents, don't go near her.

Mia is as vicious as a poisonous snake
When you press a button on her dress
She turns into a rabbit
She is half-rabbit, half-bear
She is ginger-haired
And she wears a rainbow bow.

Stay away!

Connie-Leigh Stant (10)
Harwich Community Primary School & Nursery, Harwich

Trench Killer

The Trench Killer roams through the night
Green seas will take over
Because when he sees a human trench
He lets himself inside.

Gas! A man cries out
Everyone wobbles their mask on
A man is stuck drowning
In his own blood.

Don't forget your mask
When it comes... lurking
Otherwise your inner guts will be consumed
With blood, through the night.

It will come alive
Squeeze your lungs
Until you reach home
Where you lie helpless.

Kayleigh McGinty (10)
Harwich Community Primary School & Nursery, Harwich

Oli

I can hear growls coming from under the sofa
I can smell all the food from the fridge
I can feel the blue eyes
Both of them always keeping watch
I can taste the excitement bubbling
And then he is not under the sofa.

Stood before me, he is called Oli
I can hear Oli
I can smell the food from dad's secret mini fridge
I can feel his rough white scales
I can taste happiness in the air
"You, my friendly monster,
Have caused quite the stir."

Finley Baker (10)
Harwich Community Primary School & Nursery, Harwich

The Laugh Killer

He lurks through the night
Walking through the depths of your street
Waiting for a laugh to occur
Waiting to take it away.

He'll knock on your human door
To hear it closer up
Don't let him in
Because you'll never giggle again.

How much you try, it'll never work
It's gone for life
Not one more happy sound
The Laugh Killer took it away.

But it's such a thrill
When he comes to kill
Your laugh away...

Keelee Natasha Zupan-Turner (10)
Harwich Community Primary School & Nursery, Harwich

The Night Scythe

The creature roams our town and countries
Because he is hunting Crunchies
He hides in little trenches
And kills with wrenches
He loves guns
But makes terrible puns
He acts like a magical mage
But he has been consumed with a corrupted rage
He is always grumpy
And his skin is very bumpy
He looks very vile
But he can run a mile
He hates the taste of juice
And he eats moose
He hovers above my bed
And he has slapped me in the head.

Kellan Smith (9)
Harwich Community Primary School & Nursery, Harwich

The Dream Monster

She roams through the eerie nights
Waiting for us to sleep, *zzz!*
Make sure she sees you
To say goodnight
And you will end up in her fluffy arms
Her legs are like fluffy tree stumps
Tiptoeing along the peaceful streets
She likes to hug children
She loves strawberries and grass and sweet treats
Hugs and kisses
When children are sleeping
She is praying
But don't forget
She will be back to say goodnight.

Alecia Bethany Martina Sitton (9)
Harwich Community Primary School & Nursery, Harwich

Mr Deadly

This beast, ferocious and hairy
He goes by the name Mr Deadly
He may look sweet but don't be fooled
He is very scary.

Lurking through the night he comes
Spiky and jagged fur
Sharp as a shark's tooth
You'll know who he is if you listen to this.

He lives on sweets and all things bad
Walking down the street
Knocking everything around
Crash! Don't let him in, or else...

Gracie Kadar (10)
Harwich Community Primary School & Nursery, Harwich

The Mermaid Monster

She's swimming through the misty water
Waiting for fish to eat
She gets tangled up in the fishnet
Sleeping on the water beds
Swim, swim, swim!

Out of the water, she's like a unicorn
Swimming with her rainbow tail
What a disco ball
Swim, swim, swim!

Her best friend is a unicorn
Her favourite colour is a rainbow
She was a human at first then turn to a mermaid
Swim, swim, swim!

Charlotte Kelly (9)
Harwich Community Primary School & Nursery, Harwich

But Don't Be Surprised

He's ugly but don't be surprised
He'll lure you to death with his heart and mind.

Cuddle you all day and night
But don't be surprised
He'll love you with his heart and mind.

Then he'll eat you up in seconds
Hit you with his tail
But only with one of them.

His spiky chest, thin legs
Crazy afro hair
Hard fluffy tail
Still, don't be surprised...

Natasha Eva Ford (10)
Harwich Community Primary School & Nursery, Harwich

Cute But Dangerous

He might be cute
But don't be fooled
He will take away your happiness and love.

He is really cute
He'll be really kind to you all-day
But when it comes to the night-time
Don't be fooled.

He'll eat you up in seconds
He will hit you with his scrunchies.

He will wait up for you
And wait to see if he can hear your laughter
And then take it away!

Isobelle Clay (11)
Harwich Community Primary School & Nursery, Harwich

Happy Heapy Monster

The Happy Heapy Monster
Her name is Haycali
She loves her quirky cookies
From her other crazy world
She can also be outstandingly friendly
Her crystallised blue eyes
And her craziness combined
She will hide in your closet
So beware or you will find
A crazy, happy, heaping monster
Hide as hard as you can
Watch out, keep yourself safe
Or she'll capture you too!

Maisy Murray (10)
Harwich Community Primary School & Nursery, Harwich

Pink

Hi everyone, my name is Pink
I live in a sink
I like to drink a bubbly dark pink drink
My friends tell me I need to think about how I
blink.

I am really happy
And I don't wear a nappy
I have a song
And my doorbell goes *bing bong*.

I have spider eyes
That no one identifies
Make sure you don't go to bed
In the morning, you might be dead.

Dylan Ashton Desmond (10)
Harwich Community Primary School & Nursery, Harwich

Death Killer

Tsunami crashing, monster rising
Fire breathing, water particles
Galloping noise, dinosaur trails
Bullets flying, frozen statues.

Burning trees, protecting villages
Vampire bits, dragon scales
Fire burning, all to see.

Devil haunting, nails falling
Monster uncovered, killer fights
Death comes, the legend never died
Will it still be alive, do you know?

Lilly Amanda (10)
Harwich Community Primary School & Nursery, Harwich

The Laugh Taker

Beware of this monster
Don't laugh, don't even make a peep
Don't go near him
His claws are as big as a cat's tail
Eats food as big as a globe
Legs as long as a human
He has yellow skin and fur to camouflage with the
sand.

He likes to feast on laughter
It's his best source of happiness
He can hear laughter from a mile away
Including yours!

Charlie Pearce (10)
Harwich Community Primary School & Nursery, Harwich

Furious Anger

She lies in her bed
And then turns red
Youll hear the thump
And then the bump
Thump, thump, bump!

She gets angry daily
With her sister, Baily
If she can live with you
Say boo!

She can bark
In the dark
With anger
Bark, bark, dark!

If you see fire
Getting higher
Don't worry
It's just Furious Anger.

Bryoni Maria Homatopoulos (9)
Harwich Community Primary School & Nursery, Harwich

Watermelon

In the night lurks a monster
He is green like a bean
He is red and likes to hide under your bed.

His name is Watermelon
It may sound funny
But he will steal your money
People think he is wasteful
But he is very tasteful.

He loves the smell
Of red and green blood
He likes little kids
So beware
And don't be scared!

Lydia Mcdonough (10)
Harwich Community Primary School & Nursery, Harwich

Ava

Ava, Ava
Where have you gone?
She's small like a mouse
In my huge house.

Ava, Ava
Where are you?
She's fluffy like a cat
Sat on my doormat.

Ava, Ava
What are you up to?
She's cuddly like a bunny
She might steal my money.

Ava, Ava
There you are
Sleeping in my bed
Resting your head.

Olivia Tunnicliffe (10)
Harwich Community Primary School & Nursery, Harwich

Trygon The Devil

Trygon lurks on All Hallows' Eve
Feeding on children's screams.

He has fleas
He eats trees
He only is awake on Halloween.

He is the proud ruler of the underworld
Trygon has a second head
And he never stays in bed.

His favourite words are hello, hello
"Hello, hello, bye!" he says
While he flies.

Daniel Kirk (9)
Harwich Community Primary School & Nursery, Harwich

The Nightmare Monster

She roams through your house
Waiting for you to snore
Make sure she doesn't notice you
Or you'll end up in her jaws.

Her favourite food is fish pie
And she can make you die
But when she's mad
You make her glad
Hide under your sheets
Don't make a peep
That's the end of The Nightmare Monster.

Evee Harding-Double (9)
Harwich Community Primary School & Nursery, Harwich

Angriness

A big black hole over our world
Seeks children with the wrong attitude
But if you lie
You will die.

Look out for a purple body
You can put your hand right through him
His tongue has an eye
That can spy.

So watch out, bellow
Also don't be slow
So watch out
And don't shout.

Miles Martin (9)
Harwich Community Primary School & Nursery, Harwich

Trigon!

I can hear the monstrous sounds under my bed
I can smell the blood dripping out red
I can see him killing my sister who wet the bed.

I see his yellow eyes glowing out yellow
Don't go to the loo
'Cause he will be waiting for you!

Billy Henry Sharpe (9)
Harwich Community Primary School & Nursery, Harwich

The Vampire Monster

In the dark attic
There lives a monster
I can see the blood seep out red
I can taste the blood in the air
As she eats the dead
She has big wings so she can fly high
She can catch the birds
She has long teeth to suck your blood!

Lily Sandra Grave Andrews (9)
Harwich Community Primary School & Nursery, Harwich

The Friendly Monster

Dragina is a lovely friendly monster
She cleans her wings while sitting by the river
The leaves are shivering in the breeze
We can hear the bees buzzing in the beautiful field
Buzz, buzz, buzz!

Cara-Leigh Tyler (10)
Harwich Community Primary School & Nursery, Harwich

As Silly As Can Be

C onney is a spotty boy, as funny as can be,

O n the floor, when he moves, it goes crackle,

N ice monsters are friendly like Conney,

N aughty monsters are the opposite of Conney

E ven Conney can be evil sometimes,

Y ou would be delighted to walk into his house.

I n his house is a comfy chair that feels like hair,

S ometimes when my monster is angry he goes, *grrr!*

S itting on a chair with a blanket as soft as cotton wool,

I nstead of living in a normal house, he lives in a forest,

L ove is what Conney feels all the time,

L azy monsters are like Conney,

Y oung monsters are also like Conney because Conney is only six years old.

Lexi Smith (9)

Langlands Primary School, Forfar

Monty The Monster

In the woods, I heard a frightening shriek,
It sounded like a noise that came from a crow's
beak.
I followed the sound through the trees,
Until all I heard was the buzzing of bees.

Suddenly, the beast came into view,
Then I felt the wet morning dew.
He had only one eye, that shone like a blood moon,
As the other one was a scar that never twitched,
even at noon.

His horns flicker as he feeds off fear,
When any person comes near.
His fists are rocks,
Although he feels like a teddy bear in a big, brown
box.

When you're near the monster, never boast,
Or you'll end up as burnt as toast!
His breath has an appalling smell,
It's like a witch's spell.

He sauntered closer, towards me,
I was worried he was going to have me for his tea.
Snap! He stood on a twig,
I looked up at a tree, for some reason there was a fig.

I burst out into a cold sweat,
Ever since, I've seen the monster I met.
Then, out of nowhere, there was an almighty shout,
"I am Monty the monster and I want you to get out!"

I ran home, into my bed,
I'm glad that I had fled.

Zoë McGregor (10)
Langlands Primary School, Forfar

Bob From My New Job

I started my new job,
I made a new friend, named Bob,
He had a shack in the middle of the woods,
It was old and mouldy, so I brought him some new goods.

He came out, it wasn't my friend,
It was a monster, I thought it was the end!
Electric currents ran down my spine,
Inside there were monsters drinking wine.

They all ran out, wondering what was wrong,
Screech! For some reason, they started to sing a strange song,
His hair was as pink as candyfloss,
He had his friends, but he was the boss.

He walked up to me,
I was next to a tree,
He had shape-shifted into Bob, what could I do?
He shape-shifted into a person I thought I knew.

He was terrifyingly scary and always acted nice,
He had very long horns on his tail and his back,
If you ever saw him, you would never come back.

He lived in the woods in a mouldy, old shack,
All he did was eat and was always mad,
He was my friend that turned very, very bad.

Louie Gowans (10)
Langlands Primary School, Forfar

Maverick And Jeffy

Maverick and Jeffy live under my bed,
But Jeffy plays with thread,
They're as blue as goo,
And they smell like poo.

Their eyes are as black as coal,
And Jeffy eats out of a bowl.
Their tummies gurgle like thunder,
And they murmur.

They're as angry as dogs,
They like to jump about like frogs.
Their teeth are as sharp as daggers,
And they love climbing ladders.

They're as fluffy as bunnies,
And they're really funny.
They have feet as big as a pig's,
And they love eating figs.

Every time they take a step there is a bang,
And they're in a gang,

They're in a gang called the Boo Crew,
And their shoes are new.

They love playing with bats,
And they're very fat!
They love eating pumpkins,
And their tummies are like dumplings,
They have claws,
As sharp as saws.

Jordan Walker (10)
Langlands Primary School, Forfar

Lilly The Scariest Creature On Earth

Lilly has a hard heart,
It can't wish for a dart,
She wants to be alive,
So she can hunt the beehive,
Lilly is as scary as a ghost in your house, that comes for you in the night,
But disappears when you turn on your light.

Lilly takes a stroll,
Before the eggs roll,
Lilly has a growl that is as loud as a marching band,
She wants to eat your hand,
She is as hungry as a lion that hasn't eaten for four years,
And likes to eat children's ears.

She wants to have friends but they don't speak,
Because she eats birds' beaks,
She is as sulky as a boring old teenager,
That gets herself into a lot of danger,

She has a furry cat,
That loves to eat the mat,
She has a heart like a devil,
And is a bit of a daredevil.

Jasmine Bell (10)
Langlands Primary School, Forfar

Spiky Sid

It all started at Sid's rotten house,
All mouldy with lots of lice,
Sid is my alien-looking monster,
When he has too much sugar,
He acts like a jester.

He breaks everything in sight,
And he might steal your toys in the night,
He is always ready to pounce,
And he loves cake,
When he is angry he hisses like a snake.

He wraps his wiggly four arms,
And then squeezes them until they burst,
And he has a curse -
When it turns midnight, he turns into a person,
His dad's name is Gerson.

When you leave your door open, Sid will steal
everything in your room,
And sometimes even you!
He really wants to be a Highland cow,

For this was his wish for life,
He even comes from Fife.

Jay Elder (10)
Langlands Primary School, Forfar

Looks Cute

She looks cute, like a furry teddy bear
Who loves to scare,
She has teeth as sharp as razors,
And her eyes shoot out lasers,
Her roar is as loud as a baby's scream,
And she lets off a lot of steam.

Her bow is as big as a great white shark
That you can see in the dark,
When she is annoyed, her eye fills up with redness,
Then her mind fills with angriness,
Her paws turn into claws and more and more,
She becomes an evil monster and she lets out an
almighty roar!

Leah's the colour of candyfloss,
And she loves to play darts,
But she does horrific farts,
She also loves to scare you and pull your hair,
So I would watch out,
Because she might be around the corner,
So beware.

Erin Anderson (10)
Langlands Primary School, Forfar

Nevil Naughtyman

He sneaks into schools late at night, waiting for his prey,
Once the children have entered the school,
That's when he shouts, hooray!
For when they see a glance of his fire-filled eyes,
They turn naughty, just like that,
Nevil had once turned a whole school naughty,
And all, apart from a cat.

If you smell smoke, be sure to close at least one eye,
If you don't it will make you cry,
Nevil has gooey, green skin,
He is also very thin,
Nevil is not someone you would want to meet,
Especially when you might be his next eat,
You don't want to turn naughty and cheat.

So watch out, especially if you go to school,
If you want to stay safe from Nevil Naughtyman -
follow each rule.

Holli Smith (10)
Langlands Primary School, Forfar

Silly Sam In The Forest

Silly Sam is silly like a dog that is chasing its tail,
In the forest, there is a buzz from some busy bees,
Flying around the thick, scary trees,
Laughing and giggling all day, even if he is sad.

Loaded with happiness, he strolled through the
dark, silent forest,
Yawning from exhaustion from walking for ages,
He finally had a little rest by a huge, bumpy tree.

Soon, he set off through the gloomy forest,
There was a snap from sticks breaking underneath
his feet,
That were as green as freshly-cut grass.

As he reached the end of the forest,
He was amazed that he got out,
And, at the same time, he was very relieved,
My monster is a bright, sparkling star, shooting
across the night sky.

Ashlyn Smith (10)
Langlands Primary School, Forfar

King Of The Monsters

Garry is spooky and also a little kooky,
His mouth is as big as a black hole,
He could even swallow a mole,
His teeth are sharp as razor blades,
I have seen him in many monster raids,
I want to run and scream,
But he has a monster team.
His eyes are black pools of despair,
And he has absolutely no hair,
His head is a bed of spikes and thorns,
All his legs seem to be torn,
Come to think of it, his whole body is scarred,
He shouted out, "I love lard!"
After that, he told me a story, I didn't understand,
He then said, out of nowhere, "I wish I was a
human man."

Maya McInnes (10)
Langlands Primary School, Forfar

The Slimy Monster

S uper monsters are slimy

L aughing monsters are helpful

I nteresting monsters are talented and generous

M onsters are wicked in their own way

Y ounger monsters are rough.

M onsters are always going to Mexico

O ld-fashioned monsters are scary monsters in costumes

N asty monsters are cute and fluffy

S limy monsters are happy and gooey

T houghtful monsters are loving

E vil monsters are funny and silly

R easonable monsters are sweet like sugar

S limy Sky makes a bang when she moves!

Ellie Jane Thomson (10)

Langlands Primary School, Forfar

The Big Friendly Monster

My monster's name is Shade,
When he is in the dark, he starts to fade.
He is funny and silly, he thinks his walking stick is a
time-travelling machine,
He likes to rhyme and be as clean as a bean,
He comes from Fife,
His favourite food is pizza,
He is as fast as a cheetah,
His potion is an acid that makes people better,
He likes getting a letter,
He likes walking up the steeple with his dog,
Sometimes he sees a frog,
His horns are small for his age,
He likes to be on the stage,
He likes touching thorns,
He does not like corn.

Craig Murray (10)
Langlands Primary School, Forfar

Fang Man's Night

He roams the night looking for people to scare,
Shouting "Boo!"
He does not like to wear a shoe,
He leaves a slippery trail of slime,
Every single time.
He likes to lurk in the shadows,
His favourite food is marshmallows,
When he does not get his way - he goes off in a huff,
He likes to fiddle with stuff.
When he eats he is like a pig,
And he likes to dig,
When he is drinking, he is like a dog,
He loves to hide in the fog.

Kathryn Gould (9)
Langlands Primary School, Forfar

Silly Sally

Silly Sally is as crazy as a circus clown,
Incredible Silly Sally loves to wear her pink bow,
Lovely as a humming bee,
As funny as can be,
You should never leave your door open or Silly
Sally will come.

Silly Sally is as soft as white clouds,
Adventures are Silly Sally's favourite thing to do,
Likes to be mad at times,
Lollies are her favourite food,
You can be friends with Silly Sally.

Thea Forbes (10)
Langlands Primary School, Forfar

Glay The Tall Monster

He is as tall as a 74-foot tree,
But that's what he didn't want to be.
He is as orange as an old, battered leaf,
And he loves eating peas.
He is a sabretooth tiger who kills bees,
Sometimes Glay has disgusting fleas.
When he burps it makes a big *bang!*
But when he laughs you can see his fangs.

Caitlyn Brogan (10)
Langlands Primary School, Forfar

Grumpy

The man is grumpy when he goes out at night,
He tries to save people that the monster bites.
The monster is as fast as lightning,
At night he brightens.
He is as red as a rose,
He likes to pose.
The man's eyes are so bright,
The monster sees him, gives him a fright,
And an almighty bite!

Logan Byrne (10)
Langlands Primary School, Forfar

She's Amazing

She is as bright as the sun in the sky,
Hopping like a rabbit in the field,
"Eek!" she shouts when she is scared,
She is colourful like a rainbow in the sky,
Amazing like the stars at night,
Makes the day into light,
As bright as the sun,
Zooming like a cheetah in the forest.

Wiktoria Tomaczowska (9)
Langlands Primary School, Forfar

The Stinking Stinging Monster

Beware and be aware, 'cause he doesn't like to share,
Everything is for himself, not even for a tiny elf,
His sharp and shimmering jaws are always used to break the laws,
By stealing like a thief with a mind full of mischief.

He looks like a lizard but acts like a wizard,
His hands are tiny but stretchy and slimy,
He will steal and take, the happiness people make.

He always likes to sting and it will make you stink,
He would enjoy making you ill or, most likely, he would kill,
He may sound interesting but he's vicious and never resting,
So beware and be aware, 'cause he doesn't like to share.

Mariam Enany (11)
Madni Academy, Savile Town

Bird Bud

Your normal typical monsters,
Roaming in the streets, nothing is unusual,
Except for this one.

He has an unusual liquid,
Which makes him a shape-shifter,
He has a bird potion,
Combine them together... *Boom!*

He's here... Bird Bud,
He's in the streets
Of Monster Town.

He gets laughed at,
He doesn't care what they think,
He's different from the rest.

Bushy eyebrows, long nails,
Gigantic point and a bird shape-shifter name,
The friendliest monsters make fun of him,
Less appreciation and lots of hate.

He's still there so keep your eyes open,
Be kind, get to know him

Treat him like your cousin,
Because, one day soon, he's going back to normal.

Aima Malik (9)

Madni Academy, Savile Town

No More Food! And Don't Tease Me!

Tounge McTong,
Waddling through the streets.
I don't know if you can tell,
But he always pees!

People with fries look and stare,
But all Tounge will do is cry and glare.
His spotty, dotty look gets him teased,
But he only kicks them in the knees.

Fruit salad, pineapple, mustard and chicken tikka masala,
Are the only things he eats, that'll get him larger.
His lashes are always flashing,
But his clothes are always clashing.

At the end of the day,
He always starts to play,
With the people who teased him,
Although they never made his day.

What is lying around all over the room?
Silent and asleep, not even a peep.
ABC, he runs away,
Without a backwards stare.

Fatima Malik (11)
Madni Academy, Savile Town

The Stinging Bee

As Striking moves slowly,
He will soon become the Night King,
He will sting like a bee,
And is looking for some treats,
Keep a watch out,
Because he loves some children for tea.

He roams around the night,
Waiting for children to be asleep,
Because he takes a little peep,
His legs are like tree trunks,
Stomping down the street.

His jaws open and close,
Waiting to do what he desires,
Make sure he doesn't see you,
You will get trapped between his jaws.

So watch out,
Stay under the covers,
Make sure you don't peek,
Because the evil monster is lurking around,
All the children are asleep.

Hibba Anis (10)
Madni Academy, Savile Town

Queen Monster Of Lucero

In an abandoned, old hospital,
Which no one dares to mention,
There lives the Queen of Darkness,
Beware, she roams inside.

She has hair the colour of blood,
And huge, cat-like eyes.
Her breath is as stinky as can be,
And her voice is as loud as thunder.

If anyone dares to go inside,
They will be haunted to death.
She scares with her army of ghosts,
And never takes a rest!

Who is she?
And where did she come from?
She is the Queen Monster of Lucero,
Who is well known for her crown jewels.
She roams around in this very hospital,
With her monstrous ghosts, ready to scare!

Amaara Bukhari (9)
Madni Academy, Savile Town

Jaws... Who Likes To Break Laws

Firstly, Jaws likes to break laws,
He tips bins over and eats four-leaf clovers,
He has all sorts of stupidly silly things in his head,
What are we supposed to do with hairy and
naughty Jaws?

If you tell him off, he throws a massive bin at your
head,
But he does enjoy his warm and snuggly bed.
If you threaten him, he will rip you limb by limb,
If you say something fantastic to him,
He will give you an extra sim (for your phone).

So the key point is,
To always be excellently epic,
To the law-breaking Jaws.

Aaminah Ejaz (11)
Madni Academy, Savile Town

Dark Dreams Will Come To Life

Dark dreams, spine-chilling claws,
Will pierce through your veins,
As they wiggle through your skin,
They will make you freak.

The colours will vanish,
Everything will turn black and spooky.
At the sight of him, you'll shiver,
As you're sitting, you'll feel fear.

His vivid blood eyes will make you quiver,
You'll screech but the world will be empty,
Your voice will echo through your head.

His vivid eyes will haunt you,
From ten miles away.
His claws will reach you...
Watch out!

Khadeejah Salaam (9)
Madni Academy, Savile Town

Hairy Stealer

Hi, my name is Hairy Stealer,
I like fluffy or hairy stuff,
So you better hide all of the fluff.

When I smell fluffy or hairy stuff,
I sneak to your house or wherever you are,
I will still sneak in.

When I see fluffy or hairy stuff,
With my own three eyes,
I hide behind something black,
So you can't see me!

With my two horns, I pick up anything I like,
And, if you find me anywhere in your house,
Don't forget I will give you a big scare!

Wissal Graiaouni (10)
Madni Academy, Savile Town

Minotaur Monster

I can hear a minotaur monster,
Coming to eat anything in its way,
You better run fast,
Because I've heard screams, *aargh!*

You'd better hide, quickly,
It has a gigantic mouth,
So it can gobble you up,
Quicker than you'd think.

You better go far, far away,
Because it is scary,
And has three big, green eyes.
He is terrifying because
He has a human body with a monster face.

Habiba Shah (10)
Madni Academy, Savile Town

Small But Mischievous

She's small but mischievous,
The monster you never want to meet.
She's small but mischievous,
She will never let you sleep!

If you let her play with you,
You will regret it.
'Cause when you let her play with you,
She will mess everything around!

She loves to sleep with you,
So you can get mad.
Then you'll want to pack your bags,
So she'll never be in your sight again!

Zonaira Dar (10)
Madni Academy, Savile Town

The Mood Swing Monster

In the bright summer morning,
While the shimmering sun shines without a flaw,
The Mood Swing Monster wakes up and yawns,
His sharp glistening canines as sharp as pointy claws.

He's as happy as could be,
Saying a joyous 'Hello' to everyone he passes,
He seems to be making everyone pleased,
But not for long...

Roqayyah Bint Ziaullah (10)
Madni Academy, Savile Town

The Dream Crusher

Be careful,
He's roaming the streets now,
Waiting for a beautiful, lovely dream.

He is going to find you,
Do something bad,
Something you have never had...

Oh, and don't think about opening your eyes,
Because he could be right there,
Waiting for you,
Ready to do the best he can.
Aargh!

Maryam Amankwah (10)
Madni Academy, Savile Town

Trick Or Treating

A tiny monster lurks through the night,
The lights flicker through the streetlights,
Trick-or-treaters hunting for treats,
Hoping to find lots of sweets,
The wolves howl, the owls tweet,
People in their houses stamp their feet,
The jolly children singing along to jolly songs,
Adults, angry like wild cats,
Stamp their feet on the doormat.
Flacan steals everybody's joy out of their hearts,
And wants to eat all their juicy parts,
Dogs barking at fireworks,
Flacan steals everybody's toys,
Making lots of silly noise,
Chocolate coins dropping out of people's pockets,
Flacan lurks behind, stealing,
Full of joy in his hands,
Bye-bye, trick-or-treaters, have a good night,
Now it's time to turn off the lights!

Kyle Barnett (9)
Parent Concern, Cheadle

Destroyer Madness!

Monster madness, monster madness,
He's coming for you, watch out, he might eat you,
Watch out, watch out, here he comes,
Destroyer, with his eyes, *zap, zap, zap,*
Bang! Bang! Bang!
Down go people, down go buildings,
Chew them up and spit them out,
One, two, three, trick or treat?
Here's my massive monster, sweet!

George Harrison (8)
Parent Concern, Cheadle

The Monster Who Rocks

Flishy rocks everywhere,
Sometimes giving you a scare!
His good looks turn into evil looks,
He hooks people into his little mind games,
And they always get the blame!
Watch out! He might hook you
Into his evil trap,
You might get the blame,
So don't join in with his mind games!

Alfie Moore (10)
Parent Concern, Cheadle

Spooky Man

Spooky Man had a very clever plan,
He wanted to fry people,
In his big black pan,
So he began to scare people,
And so they ran,
But he could always catch them,
In his big black pan
As he always had a scary plan,
Ha, ha, ha!

Luke Seed (10)
Parent Concern, Cheadle

All About The Mysterious Tentacle Man

He lives on Planet Fabant
And is scared of elephants.
He is tickly and funny
And as hairy as a bunny.
He never brushes his teeth,
He smells like out-of-date beef!
He lives in a bog
And a tasty feast would be a hog.
People who are terrified
Really should hide!
Fabant is a nice place,
To be fair, some monsters have a freaky face.
He jumps like crazy
And is rarely ever lazy,
His arms are really flopsy
And has a sister called Mopsy.
But beware of the scary "He",
He might find you under a tree!

Finlay Rowan (8)

St Edward's CE Primary School, Castleton

The Death Master

The Death Master is there
Under your bed
He's coming to try and eat your brain
He only comes out when it's about to rain
But if he's not there
He has shrunk down and he's in your hair
He goes in your ear
Slithers down to your tummy
And he thinks you're rather yummy
He thinks you're rather yummy
Because he eats you from the inside.

If he goes mad
He grows into a ten-foot cobra
His favourite word is sell
He gives people hell!

David Rami Erdogan (8)
St Edward's CE Primary School, Castleton

Hocus Pocus

Hocus Pocus lives in Monster Town
And he doesn't give a frown
Hocus Pocus doesn't focus
He comes out every two months on the hot days
And special days
Then he goes to the bays
He has a long tongue
And he has a big mouth
Often when he is happy, he shouts
When he is angry, he grows spots
And he eats apricots
He grows to three-foot-seven at a full moon
He will scare everyone, even a baboon!

Cole Brooks (9)
St Edward's CE Primary School, Castleton

Sid Under The Lid

I can hear sharp teeth scratching from the kitchen
I can smell the coke
I can hear something like flat duck feet
And then he is not in the kitchen
But stood before me, he is called Sid
I can hear Sid laughing
I can smell the peas and Coke
Too many peas and he turns green
Needs bathing
Sid is in a cloak
If he sees you, he will poke.

Keona Chiwanda (8)
St Edward's CE Primary School, Castleton

Bon Bon, Watch Out

Bon Bon lives under a tree
And she has a friend called Bree
Bon Bon comes out at Easter
And celebrates by eating
Special Easter eggs
Bon Bon is tiny tiny small
And when she's scared, she curls up into a ball
But she's not always kind
I think you will find
Bon Bon steals children's Easter eggs
So if you see her, beg!

Lexie Rae Kathleen Mcgarry (8)
St Edward's CE Primary School, Castleton

Hog From The Bog

If you go to the toilet at night
You might feel a fright
Hiding in there is a monster with furry hair
When you switch on the light
He pops out like a kite
His name is Hog
From the bog
He has a big mouth with no teeth to be found
Beware
He might be over there...

Lewis Pattinson (8)

St Edward's CE Primary School, Castleton

Stretch-Kin In The Kitchen

She is stretchy, small
As big as a football
She stretches long, far and wide
But you can't see her when she hides
You'll find her in the fridge behind the cheese
If you want some
You'll have to say please!

Kelis Idaewor-Knox (8)
St Edward's CE Primary School, Castleton

Nightwing's Magical Job

Night wing flies like an angel and lands gently on a
soft cloud,
Her job is important which makes her very proud,
Her horns glow like stars in the sky, she's so
graceful like a butterfly.
She is clever at camouflage and hiding from
grownups
Her fur changes colour to fit with wallpaper -from
trucks to ducks
When children are sleeping she gets rid of bad
dreams
Her horns use their magic before children scream
Her sharp fangs like razors crunch the nightmares
away
When the children wake up they have a happy day
As quick as a flash she flies through the night,
happy again that she won the fight
Nightwing is lovely and kind and not scary,
Even though she has horns, razor teeth and is a
little bit hairy!

Libby Wade (9)
St. Peter's Primary School, South Croydon

Behind The Bushes

Who's that monster behind those bushes?
He's trying to search for where the wood is.
Howling and growling in the midst of noon,
He'll come for you when there's a full moon.
With yellow spiky teeth and orange cool shades,
He's lonely in Chompsville, he needs your aid.
His soft green fur is where he gets his name,
He's good at sports and a quick ball game.

Sometimes he's lazy, sometimes keen,
Sometimes calm, sometimes mean.
Luckily I visited Mr McFluff,
I went to his house and saw all his cool stuff.
We went to a store and visited next door.
It was such a great day, I went on to say,
"Goodbye, Mr McFluff!"

Hannah Ebrahim (11)
Ummul Mumineen Academy, Grangetown

Monsters Everywhere?

Monsters, monsters, under my bed.
Monsters, monsters, stuck in my head.
Monsters, monsters, make my teeth chatter
Monsters, monsters, my mum says no matter.
Monsters, monsters don't even dare!
Monsters, monsters, if you do
I will pull out your hair!

Zaynah Miznah Hussein (8)
Ummul Mumineen Academy, Grangetown

My Monster

My monster comes out at midnight
She sometimes likes to fight
She has a big vicious bite
Which can give you quite a fright.

My monster is very very scary
Her head and her body are hairy
Sometimes she wishes she was a fairy
Because her breath smells of gone-off dairy.

My monster likes to be caring
She is super daring
Sometimes she is magically sharing
The best and funniest thing she can do is her glaring.

Katie Cheesman (8)
Yarm School, Yarm

The Cookie Monster

The Cookie Monster loves cookies
He will creep into your house when you're still at
school
He devours all the cookies in your house
The Cookie Monster is never full
He even looks like a cookie
He sneaks out of the house
Before you are home
If you see him, he will always say hi
Children always like him
But for some strange reason
Adults are scared of him.

Edie Redhead Sweeney (8)
Yarm School, Yarm

Halloween Monster

It was a cold, dark October night
All the children were excited for Halloween
Getting ready to trick or treat
To choose the outfit to make everyone scream
Leaving the house, all dressed up
I looked up at the stars that were shining so bright
They looked like diamonds in the sky
Lighting up the dark streets where I was
Hiding around the corner, waiting to say hi.

I have sharp pointy ears and sharp pointy teeth
I might look scary with my one red eye
However, I'm really nice underneath
You won't hear me coming, you won't hear a peep
Even though I'm clumsy, I have silent feet
I would like to be your friend
I would like to make you smile
This Halloween night, let's go trick or treating in
style
Scaring all the children in my cyclops suit
Let's run around the houses and have a real hoot!

Grace Broe (8)
Ysgol Gymraeg Bro Allta, Ystrad Mynach

Jessie, The Messy Monster

Jessie is a monster only I can see,
Which means the blame for the mess is always on me.
She eats bobbles for breakfast and socks for tea,
And is always leaving a mess around me.
Mum cleans the house, sorting out my stuff,
Only to find odd socks, she goes in a huff!
She does make me laugh, oh what a joy!
Mum thinks Jessie is just a fluffy toy.
Clothes, food, all over the floor,
It's surprisingly messy, I'm needing to clean up more.
Mornings are the best,
After Jessie's had her rest.
I hear giggles in my bed,
While Mum looks for bobbles, scratching her head.
Bathtime gets rather crazy,
Even though she's lazy.
She loves *whooshing* the water, side to side,

Pretending she's on a log flume ride.
My favourite of all is at night,
When my monster Jessie snuggles me tight.
I can feel her fluffy fur, all soft like a cloud,
And I listen to the purring snore getting loud.

Elena Bilenki (8)

Ysgol Gymraeg Bro Allta, Ystrad Mynach

My Ugly Monsters

There were two ugly monsters
That soon became friends
They would come out in the night
And drive me around the bend
The two little monsters were pink, purple and blue
They were always very excited
Always shouting, "Woo hoo!"
Mummy and Daddy didn't know about my
monsters
They would be asleep in bed
But if I told them about my friends
They would say it was just in my head
Snotty and Stinky were their names
And during the night, we would play games
They were fast as lightning
Smelt like rotten cheese
But they were my friends
So excuse them please
When I grew older
My monsters went away

But in my memory, Snotty and Stinky
Will always stay and play.

Abigail Roberts (8)

Ysgol Gymraeg Bro Allta, Ystrad Mynach

Nightmare Monster

I am the nightmare monster,
I creep in late at night,
I turn good dreams to bad ones,
To give you a big fright.

I'll fill them up with spiders,
And creepy crawlies too,
And ghosts and ghouls and goblins,
And monsters that go *boo!*

I'll tell you a little secret,
I feed on children's fear,
So when you're not afraid anymore,
Then I will disappear.

I'll move on to the next child,
And wait till they're in bed,
I'll go into their peaceful dreams,
And fill them up with dread.

So next time you are sleeping,
And you start dreaming too,

Just know the nightmare monster,
Is coming to get you!

Jac Davies (8)
Ysgol Gymraeg Bro Allta, Ystrad Mynach

There's A Monster In My Wardrobe!

There's a monster in my wardrobe!
I've seen him! Yes! He's there,
With one black, robotic arm,
And bubblegum-blue hair.

There's a monster in my wardrobe!
He's big and red and round,
His six beady eyes are watching,
When I am sleeping sound.

There's a monster in my wardrobe!
His one leg is a spring,
He bounces like a bunny,
It's the most amazing thing!

There's a monster in my wardrobe!
Springzilla is his name,
Scaring children in the night,
Is his terrifying game.

There's a monster in my wardrobe!
He's there when I'm in bed,
Is there a monster in my wardrobe?
Or is he in my head?

Heulyn Philip Webb Price (8)
Ysgol Gymraeg Bro Allta, Ystrad Mynach

My Monster Friend

My monster is not horrible or grumpy, but
sometimes scary.
He has two big front teeth and moon-shaped eyes,
but he's not the least bit hairy.
He's as fast as lightning,
Which can sometimes be frightening.
His four arms help him to climb walls,
Which help him to reach heights to listen for calls.
You know who my monster is by his lightning bolt
eye,
He comes out to play when the moon is in the sky.
He likes to be smart and wears a bow tie,
He gives it a spin when it's time to say goodbye.
He's really a secret and only I can see him,
Sometimes, I wish that I could be him.
We make up stories and draw pictures together,
I hope he's my friend forever and ever.

Elektra Clarke (7)
Ysgol Gymraeg Bro Allta, Ystrad Mynach

Drake, The Famous Snake

My monster looks like a bit of a snake,
I decided to call him big, bad Drake.
He's got lots of colours, but he is really mean,
When he gets angry, he goes mad green.
He's big, bites and snarls, he is really scary,
His belly is fat and really hairy.
He shouts and screams when I am about,
All he eats is fresh trout.
He goes in the loch that's called the Ness,
He's famous around the world and not any less.
Some don't believe me when I say he's a mate,
We're even so close, we've been on a date.

But he doesn't like strangers so he might not see you,
That's my monster poem, nice to meet you.

Dylan Rourke (9)
Ysgol Gymraeg Bro Allta, Ystrad Mynach

Scary Night

When I went to bed
Strange thoughts went through my head
That a monster had invaded my room
A shadow appeared
With bolts for ears
With a face as green as The Hulk
He wore a red coat
And had feet as large as a boat
And skin as rough as bark
He grunted and growled
The noise was so loud
The room began to shake
I froze in fright
This was a terrible night
But was it all a dream?
This hairy monster I'd seen
With eyes as wide as the moon
"Please go away, you're too scary to stay
I just want to go to sleep!"
I peeped out from the covers

The coast was clear
Phew, no more monsters were here!

Dylan Teconi (8)
Ysgol Gymraeg Bro Allta, Ystrad Mynach

Coolie The Monster Under My Bed

My monster called Coolie lives under my bed
He loves to play and is fluffy and red
He likes to play football and colouring in
I really think he is my long lost twin
He sneaks downstairs to get me some Pringles
And when he comes back, I give him some tickles
He eats lots of Pringles and goes on my iPad
I hear him on YouTube watching Chad
He hides in my rucksack when we go cycling
We go off-road and he finds it frightening
We go really fast and he always falls out
I carry on cycling and he gives me a shout
That is a story about my monster called Coolie
But in fact it's about my grandpa Tony.

Harrison Gray Martin (8)

Ysgol Gymraeg Bro Allta, Ystrad Mynach

Lola The Quatropus

Lola is a quatropus,
It's kind of like an octopus,
Except she has four legs, not eight,
Which means she's always running late,
Her three eyes sparkle and glitter,
As monsters go, she couldn't be prettier,
There's no need to be scared of her
Lola doesn't growl, it's more of a purr,
She lets you stroke her, her fur is smooth as silk,
Her favourite treats are seaweed and milk,
The game she likes to play is quatropus tag,
We play all day long while running zig-zag,
When the sun goes down and it's time to sleep,
Lola the quatropus doesn't peep.

Cariad Morgan (7)
Ysgol Gymraeg Bro Allta, Ystrad Mynach

Steve The Shape-Shifter

Steve is a slippery, slimy monster
He slides along the floor and his tentacles get
longer
His eight enormous sticky pads
Will gather all your treats
Beware Steve The Shape-Shifter
He's difficult to beat!

His eyes are square and triangular
His spikes are as sharp as swords
His hair is as bright as a beacon
His teeth are as sharp as Jaws!

Steve shifts sluggishly and likes changing shape
He blows up into a bubble
Then pops into a snake
He lives under the bikesheds
A dark and soggy place
He comes out at night-time
And shows his ugly face!

Llewelyn Cribb (8)
Ysgol Gymraeg Bro Allta, Ystrad Mynach

The Monster In The Room

What did I see?
Was it real or was it a nightmare?
I don't know, but I'm sure I see it there,
It was in my room but I don't know whom,
It looked so ugly and I bet it wasn't very snuggly,
It was lime and covered in slime,
He was very hairy and looked so scary.
I felt terrified and was trembling,
It was so fat it must have eaten a feast to be such
a large beast,
It made a chilling sound as he frowned,
It sounded like a howl and it's breath smelt really
foul.
I closed my eyes, hoping he would leave,
And when I opened my eyes I felt relieved,
He was gone.

Elan Davies (9)
Ysgol Gymraeg Bro Allta, Ystrad Mynach

Lala The Monster

Her eyes are like a ball of fire,
She loves climbing up and down the wire.
As soon as the sun goes down,
This monster is roaming around.

Lala has a very special feature,
She wobbles like an octopus,
Her long and spiky tongue is venomous,
That kills bullies on the campus.

This scary monster can be invisible,
Can be felt in the air but not tangible,
She can fly as high as the sky,
And sometimes she disguises a baby's cry.

So watch out if you are naughty,
'Cause Lala has eyes that only you can see.

Kyle Gittings (7)
Ysgol Gymraeg Bro Allta, Ystrad Mynach

Mysterious Monster

There is a monster hiding under my bed
Tall and slimy, his skin is dark red
His feet are so furry, also so smelly
His belly is big, wobbly like jelly.

He looks very friendly and not so scary
His hands are big, his knuckles are hairy
He likes to tell jokes, he's very funny
He likes to read stories and has a toy bunny.

There is a monster hiding under my bed
"Please don't be scared," the monster said
"I'm not scary, I want to be friends,
I will protect you until night-time ends."

Caitlin Elizabeth Bosher-Lewis (9)
Ysgol Gymraeg Bro Allta, Ystrad Mynach

Mushy The Crisp-Munching Monster

Mushy is a Crisp-Munching monster,
He is hairy, not scary,
He is not naughty, he is nice,
He is loud, not quiet,
He enjoys munching crisps, all through the night!
He is pretty messy, always full of crumbs,
Pickled onion crisps are his favourite, you can hear him scream, "Yum yum!"
He leaves a trail of crumbs wherever he has been,
Then uses his long tongue, to lick the carpet clean.
Do not be scared of Mushy, he is a fluffy, funny beast,
He has no scary horns or fangs - he just loves his crisp-munching midnight feast!

Osian Evans (8)

Ysgol Gymraeg Bro Allta, Ystrad Mynach

The Sock Monster

My mum says there's a sock monster,
Living in our house,
If he does live here,
He must be as quiet as a mouse.

My mum says he must be very small,
Because we've never seen him in the house before,
I imagine he is bouncy, as bouncy as a ball,
And that he is fluffy, pink and small.

I think he is quite stinky,
After eating all the socks,
We search high and low,
But Fluffy must be as sneaky as a fox.

Pink ones, fluffy ones,
Blue ones, comfy ones,
Our sock monster loves them all!

Seren Croll (8)
Ysgol Gymraeg Bro Allta, Ystrad Mynach

Sandy Andy

Sandy Andy lives on a beach
This is a story I have to teach
Sit down and relax your feet.
Together we will learn
How to keep the beach neat.

Body like a never-ending worm
Four arms, a thousand legs,
They all look like little pegs
Sandy Andy likes to help build sandcastles,
Sandy likes to play in the sea,
Sandy will get you candy!

If you want him to do all this
Make sure you don't leave any rubbish
Because even if you are scared of fish
He will eat you like a tasty dish!

Aidan Lloyd Williams (8)
Ysgol Gymraeg Bro Allta, Ystrad Mynach

The Slug That Was Slow And Fat

Slugish the walking slug is slimy and small,
He has four legs and he walks proud and tall,
He sleeps all day and hunts at night,
Don't disturb him because he'll give you a fright.
He'll hide in the garden, eating all the greens,
It's easy to see where he's been,
He eats all night until he can't anymore,
Sometimes he can't even fit through the door.
He goes back to his bed before morning begins,
He stays there all day until it's time to do it all over again.

Gethin Marsh (9)
Ysgol Gymraeg Bro Allta, Ystrad Mynach

Gruff And My Pile Of Stuff

I can see a pile of great big stuff
All my favourite toys
I sigh again as I see
Gruff has been at my stuff.

He's big and tall and mighty strong
He's always scaring my sisters
They don't see he likes to play
And then get scared and run away.

He isn't scary or loud or lairy
But just very hairy
Poor old Gruff
He is just a big ball of fluff.

I hope one day I can say,
"Thank you Gruff
For playing with my pile of stuff."

Imogen Wivell (8)
Ysgol Gymraeg Bro Allta, Ystrad Mynach

Furry Fred

Monsters hiding in my room,
Behind the wardrobe and under my bed,
Creeping and crawling,
His eyes are all red.

Monsters hiding in my room,
Fat and furry with three eyes,
One-toothed wonder,
He ate all the pies!

Monster hiding in my room,
Gloopy, green snot glowing,
Scratching and snuffling,
Stinky, loud burps blowing.

Monster hiding in my room,
Get back down the garden, into the shed,
You'll never scare me,
My furry monster Fred!

Logan Barwood (9)
Ysgol Gymraeg Bro Allta, Ystrad Mynach

Slimy And The Stars

Slimy is my best friend
He lives behind my shed
Some monsters are tall
Some monsters are small
My monster is not very big at all
Slimy sits in my garden
We look up at the stars
We do this every night
And see them shining bright
When we look up to the sky
We see them shooting by
We ooo and ahh and gaze at them
As they light up the sky
We make a wish and sing a song
Slimy starts to yawn
He says goodnight, see you soon
As now it's nearly dawn.

Kian John Kevan Inseal (8)
Ysgol Gymraeg Bro Allta, Ystrad Mynach

Mixed Up Friendship

I went on a walk on an autumn day
I passed a pond on my way
I saw a creature that was pink
And it gave me a wink
The creature wore a dress
And it was not a mess
I walked up and said, "Hi!"
And she said, "Do you want some pie?
I am a monster, please don't run
Stay here and have some fun
I am kind, cute and friendly
Just like you
Let's sit down and enjoy the view
Now you are my friend
The story has to come to an end!"

Lilly-May Sullivan (8)
Ysgol Gymraeg Bro Allta, Ystrad Mynach

Billy The Hairy Monster

In the deep, dark wood,
From a deep, dark hole,
Out pops
One pointy nose with a blue, shiny spot,
Two bulging, green, scary eyes,
Three large, hairy ears,
Four sticky fingers with long, sharp nails,
Five dangly, bristly legs, each with
Six slimy toes,
Seven grey, rotten teeth that drip like a tap and
Eight humongous purple spikes, right along his
back.

What can it be?
Argh! It's Billy the hairy monster!
He's come to eat our tea.

Elisa Ruth Poole (8)
Ysgol Gymraeg Bro Allta, Ystrad Mynach

Snobey The Monster

Snobey is his name
He likes playing games
He's blue and purple, like a turtle
Snobey has a boyfriend called Toby
He's hard as a nail and tiny as a snail
He's soft and gentle and experimental
He's hairy and ever so scary
He likes to cuddle and jump in enormous puddles
His eyes are different
He is magnificent
He likes to have fun and play in the sun
He is gentle but ever so mental
Don't be shy
Just say hi to Snobey the monster.

Evie-Louise Corns (8)

Ysgol Gymraeg Bro Allta, Ystrad Mynach

Apricot Gum

Monsters are scary,
Some of them are cool,
Even if they sometimes
Follow you to school.

Sat in my classroom,
I heard a strange sound,
Something was behind me,
It made me look around.

The monster was a giant,
With six blistered legs,
All of his body
Was held together with pegs.

I thought I might ask him,
What his name might be,
He said it was "Apricot Gum,
But my friends call me AG!"

Morgan Daniel (9)
Ysgol Gymraeg Bro Allta, Ystrad Mynach

Shadows On The Wall

M onsters, monsters everywhere
O ver here, over there, everyone beware
N o! Please don't come near me
S tay over there, I don't want to see
"T rust me," he says
E ars prick up, I turn my head
R eally, did that monster just speak?
S hadows get closer, I don't want to peek.

"G oodnight," says my dad
O ff to sleep I go, my monster's not bad!

Phoebe Holland (8)
Ysgol Gymraeg Bro Allta, Ystrad Mynach

Alice, The Friendly Monster

Meet Alice, she's a monster, as fluffy as a cloud,
No yellow, scary eyes or claws, just friendly and not too loud.
Don't be terrified, don't run and hide,
Alice is here to make you happy and smile.
So, next time you feel a little bit afraid of what's under your bed,
Just think of Alice and have happy thoughts in your head.
The idea of a monster to you might be ugly and unkind,
But Alice is a very good monster friend of mine.

Isabelle Louise McBride (9)

Ysgol Gymraeg Bro Allta, Ystrad Mynach

My Monster

My scary monster is big and red
His name is Night Crawler
But he always likes being in his bed.

He has twelve spiky horns
And three eyes in his head
With huge wide wings
And sharp claws that are red.

My monster likes eating
And makes a mess on the mats
But one of his favourites
Is the neighbourhood cats.

My scary monster wants to live by the sea
And wants to scare as many people as can be.

Ioan Roberts (8)

Ysgol Gymraeg Bro Allta, Ystrad Mynach

The Feared Monster

Fluffy Stitches is a monster
Who lives under my bed,
She likes to roam around at night,
And fills my mam with dread.

She messes with her make-up,
And leaves stuff lying around,
She even hides her straighteners,
They're still nowhere to be found.

To Mam, she's just a monster,
But to me, she's my best friend.
She's always there to make me smile,
Our fun just never ends.

Carys Rhianwen Mair Davies (8)
Ysgol Gymraeg Bro Allta, Ystrad Mynach

Money Monster

M y favourite monster sits

O n a pile of money

N ever shouts or hits

E ats coins and paper

Y ikes! I love him to bits.

M y mother doesn't think it's funny

O nly because he takes

N early all her money

S ometimes, the money monster will

T reat us all with money

E verywhere he goes

R andom coins appear! Hooray!

Harri Ap Llwyd Dafydd (7)

Ysgol Gymraeg Bro Allta, Ystrad Mynach

Ox And His Socks

I have this little monster,
Who goes by the name of Ox,
He has this little problem,
He likes to eat my socks.

Stripy ones, spotty ones,
It really does not matter,
But if you ask him, dirty or clean?
I think he'd prefer the latter.

Now Ox is a funny little character,
Who likes to play tricks,
So when it's time to do the laundry,
He replaces my socks with bricks.

Lexie Cox (7)
Ysgol Gymraeg Bro Allta, Ystrad Mynach

Battles In The Night!

One night, there were two monsters
That were destroying houses,
An accident by one, purposeful by the other.
One was very mean,
And was not very clean.
The other was very kind,
As he had a very smart mind.
They carried on battling, all through the night,
By the time the morning came, it was very bright.
Gadynunus the monster had won the day,
The country was safe for children to play.

Dylan D'Cruz (7)
Ysgol Gymraeg Bro Allta, Ystrad Mynach

Stinky Stella

She smells like fish and nappies
She's always very happy
But where she lives, you would not guess
Her home is always in a mess
It's where we put unwanted food
So if she did not eat it, that would be rude
With a chubby belly shaped like a ball
It's easy for Stella to have a fall
She waddles like a penguin
Yes, you guessed it,
Stinky Stella lives in the bin.

Abi-Mai Yendle (8)
Ysgol Gymraeg Bro Allta, Ystrad Mynach

Frank Who Stank

There once was a monster called Frank,
He grew to the size of a tank,
He had great big fangs which were pointy and
scary,
And his breath was green and stank.

Frank slept all day and came out at night,
And crept into children's rooms to give them a
fright.
The only way you would know he'd been there,
Was the stench of his breath he'd leave in the air.

Lucas Owen Yeo (8)
Ysgol Gymraeg Bro Allta, Ystrad Mynach

The Eating Monster

My name is Joey the monster,
And I eat everything in sight,
I go to sleep all day,
And I am awake all through the night.

I'm big, fluffy and green,
And also I look very mean,
My favourite is chicken and chips,
And I like to dance and wiggle my hips.

So when I'm around, keep everything out of sight,
Or you will see me take a big bite.

Joseph Anthony Gill (8)
Ysgol Gymraeg Bro Allta, Ystrad Mynach

My Monster, Ugg

I've got a monster called Ugg
Who lives under my bed
Ugg's tongue is bright yellow
And his hair is bright red
Now Ugg isn't scary
He likes to have a joke
He tried cooking toast one day
And filled the house with smoke
He tried to paint my bedroom
But got paint everywhere
So now Ugg has a bright red tongue
And bright yellow hair!

Ben Tomas Watkins (8)
Ysgol Gymraeg Bro Allta, Ystrad Mynach

Frank The Four-Eyed Freak

We like to play a prank
On our big friend called Frank
When Frank went to the bank
A man in the bank
Thought Frank stank
Frank's house looked like a mouse
Frank came home from the bank
Because he stank
He went and washed himself in his fish tank
Frank The Four-Eyed Freak
He is such a geek
And a master of playing hide-and-seek.

Mali Dummett (8)
Ysgol Gymraeg Bro Allta, Ystrad Mynach

Snakeyla

Snakeyla lives in the jungle,
She eats her favourite food called 'mungle',
She slithers about, looking for trouble,
She bites you with venom, you grow like a bubble,
She is fast like the wind,
You'd better watch out!
She does backflips and front-flips,
And artistry too!
Snakelya is naughty,
So enter the jungle, if you dare!

Harlow Amelia Nicholas (7)
Ysgol Gymraeg Bro Allta, Ystrad Mynach

Disguise

Eyecorn is a unicorn in disguise,
Her colours sparkle like the warm summer sea,
Her smell is as strong as a summer meadow,
Her horn is as proud as the Eiffel Tower,
But, a monster they call her!
A three-eyed monster!
Her ugly vision will catch you in her gaze,
And her monster powers will always amaze,
Eyecorn - a monster master of disguise!

Ffion Francis (8)
Ysgol Gymraeg Bro Allta, Ystrad Mynach

Fluff The Sock Stealer

There once was a monster called Fluff,
big eyes, wide mouth, with a tail like a powder puff,
so squidgy and soft but stinks so much of cheese,
he makes me wheeze,
forever watching the clocks,
waiting, as quiet as a mouse, to steal your socks,
time to learn a lesson - put your socks in the drawer,
as Fluff will steal what's left on the floor.

Leila-Jo Powell (9)
Ysgol Gymraeg Bro Allta, Ystrad Mynach

Jeremy And Me

Jeremy's my friend who lives in my head
We're best friends when I go to bed
When I fall asleep I see him eating some meat
From a large green bin
He's friendly and fun like a newly-bought puppy
He keeps me company so I never need to worry
When I wake up, Jeremy's gone
But there's no need to worry, he'll be back later on.

Blaidd Carwyn Clifford (8)
Ysgol Gymraeg Bro Allta, Ystrad Mynach

Jumbo The Monster

Jumbo's tummy is hungry,
He will strike tonight,
We hear a grumble, we know we are right.

His horns are big and sharp,
He will easily rip my watermelon apart.

He eats all the food in the house,
Which causes him to fart.

In the morning, my dad turns into a nutter,
He is big and hairy and left fur in the butter.

Abigail Lucy Brown (9)
Ysgol Gymraeg Bro Allta, Ystrad Mynach

Monster

In the middle of the night,
I like to take flight,
And see what adventures are ahead.
Fun and mischief
As naughty as can be,
Fill my night with so much glee.
Big, pink and fluffy
I always like to play,
In dark places is where I like to stay.
Scaring and teasing is what I do best,
Making new friends is the best thing I guess!

Aimee Harris (9)
Ysgol Gymraeg Bro Allta, Ystrad Mynach

What Is A Monster?

What is a monster?
Does anyone really know?
Are they big and ugly
And have eyes that really glow?

Do they hide around corners
Or underneath our beds?
Are they trying to scare us
Or asking to be fed?

Who has seen these monsters
That give us such a fright?
Maybe they're around us
Hiding in plain sight.

Olivia Morris-Brown (8)
Ysgol Gymraeg Bro Allta, Ystrad Mynach

Billy The One-Eyed Monster

Fanged teeth, silk-furred,
He's a very friendly beast
That sits on the stairs with his size ten feet.
He likes to watch you eat your food,
With his one big eye,
Green, orange, yellow and red,
Hoping for a bite.
Billy the one-eyed monster,
With two horns upon his head,
His favourite food is Nutella chocolate spread.

Amelia Angel (7)
Ysgol Gymraeg Bro Allta, Ystrad Mynach

Animal Laynion

Animal Laynion is his name
Al for short if it's all the same
He lives on a planet far from Wales
'Animal Kryptonians', say all the tales
He's a general for the Kryptonian soldiers
He casts a spell with deadly boulders
He has wings, laser eyes and bionic ears,
And an axe on his feet to wield extra fear.

Thomas Clutton (8)
Ysgol Gymraeg Bro Allta, Ystrad Mynach

The Welsh Dragon Monster

My monster has eyes like rugby balls
It has teeth like spikes of the stadium
Its mouth is like an open rooftop
Its claws are like the Welsh rugby pack
Its body is as big as Cardiff city centre
Its tail flicks like George North scoring a try
It sits silently waiting to catch its prey
Then blows fire to win the day.

Iolo Anthony (8)
Ysgol Gymraeg Bro Allta, Ystrad Mynach

Frosty The Snow Monster

She has blue eyes
She makes snow and ice
She's a friendly monster
And her fur feels nice.

When you see her
She'll quietly say,
"I'm a friendly monster
Don't run away!"

So throw a snowball
She wants to play
Building a snowman
You'll have a great day.

Lois Poole (8)
Ysgol Gymraeg Bro Allta, Ystrad Mynach

Odyssey The Three-Eyed Monster

His arms were long and wiggly
His horns were sharp and prickly
He only came out at night
To give you a little fright
His three eyes went different directions
So he could see your exact location
His fangs were small and mighty
His claws were long and pointy
He was Odyssey the three-eyed monster.

Dylan Jones (8)
Ysgol Gymraeg Bro Allta, Ystrad Mynach

Ugly Monster

There once was a monster so tall and hairy,
He had big, red eyes and was ever so scary,
He was big and fat, with long, sharp claws,
And a mouth full of teeth as sharp as Jaws',
He banged and stamped whenever he walked,
And growled and dribbled whenever he talked.

Tieghan White (9)
Ysgol Gymraeg Bro Allta, Ystrad Mynach

Jeff The Monster

Jeff is very fat and scary
And he has a friend called Meri
Jeff and Meri like to go to the park
Their favourite is the merry-go-round
They have pizza every time
When they went on the merry-go-round
They found a pound
They go to the park and scare kids.

Niamh Protheroe
Ysgol Gymraeg Bro Allta, Ystrad Mynach

Monster FC

My name is the Furry Forward,
And football is my game.
One day, I'll be famous,
And everyone will know my name.

I play as a striker,
And fast as lightning.
But though I'm a monster,
I'm never frightening.

William Chant (7)
Ysgol Gymraeg Bro Allta, Ystrad Mynach

Attack Of The Mystery Zombie

It was a very dark night
And there was a monster ready to fright
He roams around and wants your blood
If you see him, run
Don't act like you're stuck in mud
You've been warned
Beware of The Mystery Zombie!

Lennon Hughes (8)
Ysgol Gymraeg Bro Allta, Ystrad Mynach

My Friend, Mike

There once was a monster called Mike
Who liked to ride his bike
He had arms and legs too
He was spiky and hairy
And smelt like poop
He may do all the things above
But he always shows me his love.

Taylor Jay Jones (8)
Ysgol Gymraeg Bro Allta, Ystrad Mynach

The Frightening Monster

There once was a monster called Fred
Who lived at the end of my bed
He came out in the night
And gave me a fright
But he was gone before it was light!

Mia Saunders (8)

Ysgol Gymraeg Bro Allta, Ystrad Mynach

Steel Strike

Tongue flick
Prey detected
Silent slither
Lightning strike
Strong coils
Suffocating
Last gasp
Stomach full for another day.

Nathaniel Sears (8)
Ysgol Gymraeg Bro Allta, Ystrad Mynach

Billy And Bob

Billy is slimy and lots of fun
He likes to wobble around the town
Pink in colour and one blue eye
He sticks out his tongue, he isn't shy!

Summer Cushing (8)

Ysgol Gymraeg Bro Allta, Ystrad Mynach

YOUNG WRITERS INFORMATION

We hope you have enjoyed reading this book – and that you will continue to in the coming years.

If you're a young writer who enjoys reading and creative writing, or the parent of an enthusiastic poet or story writer, do visit our website **www.youngwriters.co.uk**. Here you will find free competitions, workshops and games, as well as recommended reads, a poetry glossary and our blog. There's lots to keep budding writers motivated to write!

If you would like to order further copies of this book, or any of our other titles, then please give us a call or order via your online account.

Young Writers
Remus House
Coltsfoot Drive
Peterborough
PE2 9BF
(01733) 890066
info@youngwriters.co.uk

Join in the conversation!
Tips, news, giveaways and much more!

 YoungWritersUK   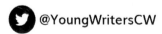 @YoungWritersCW